Activities We Do

We Celebrate Holidays

by Connor Stratton

FOCUS READERS
SCOUT

www.focusreaders.com

Focus Readers is distributed by North Star Editions:
sales@northstareditions.com | 888-417-0195

Produced for Focus Readers by Red Line Editorial.

Photographs ©: kali9/iStockphoto, cover, 1; Tom Wang/Shutterstock Images, 4; wavebreakmedia/Shutterstock Images, 7; RyanJLane/iStockphoto, 9 (top), 16 (top right); iofoto/Shutterstock Images, 9 (bottom); bowdenimages/iStockphoto, 11 (top), 16 (bottom right); andresr/iStockphoto, 11 (bottom); Rawpixel/iStockphoto, 13 (top); SolStock/iStockphoto, 13 (bottom); lisegagne/iStockphoto, 15, 16 (bottom left); Veronika Sekotova/Shutterstock Images, 16 (top left)

Library of Congress Cataloging-in-Publication Data
Names: Stratton, Connor, author.
Title: We celebrate holidays / by Connor Stratton.
Description: Lake Elmo, MN : Focus Readers, [2020] | Series: Activities we do | Audience: Grades: K to grade 3. | Includes index.
Identifiers: LCCN 2019009611 (print) | LCCN 2019012976 (ebook) | ISBN 9781641859912 (pdf) | ISBN 9781641859349 (ebook) | ISBN 9781641857963 (hardcover) | ISBN 9781641858656 (pbk.)
Subjects: LCSH: Holidays--Juvenile literature.
Classification: LCC GT3933 (ebook) | LCC GT3933 .S75 2020 (print) | DDC 394.26--dc23
LC record available at https://lccn.loc.gov/2019009611

Printed in the United States of America
Mankato, MN
May, 2019

About the Author

Connor Stratton enjoys celebrating holidays, eating popcorn, and watching movies with friends. He lives in Minnesota.

Table of Contents

Holidays Are Fun

We have many holidays.

They are fun.

We like to celebrate.

We celebrate the New Year.

We stay up late.

We have a party.

Celebrating People

We celebrate
Valentine's Day.
We make **hearts**.
We make cards.

heart

card
Mom
XOXO
XO

We celebrate Mother's Day.

We celebrate Father's Day.

We honor our **parents**.

mother

father

Holiday Eating

We celebrate Halloween.

We dress up.

We eat **candy**.

candy

We celebrate Thanksgiving.

We spend time with family.

We eat lots of **food**.

Glossary

candy

hearts

food

parents

Index